Free Spirit, Free Spirit Publishing, and associated logos
are trademarks and/or registered trademarks of Free
Spirit Publishing Inc. A complete listing of trademarks is
available at www.freespirit.com.

Library of Congress Cataloging-in-Publication Data
Feigh, Alison.
    On those runaway days / by Alison Feigh ; illustrated
by Laura Logan.
        p. cm.
    ISBN-13: 978-1-57542-286-2
    ISBN-10: 1-57542-286-7
 1. Runaway children—Juvenile literature. I. Logan,
Laura. II. Title.
    HV713.F45 2008
    362.74—dc22
                      2007044249

Edited by John Kober
Cover and interior design by Michelle Lee

10 9 8 7 6 5 4 3 2 1
Printed in China

Free Spirit Publishing Inc.
217 Fifth Avenue North, Suite 200
Minneapolis, MN 55401-1299
(612) 338-2068
help4kids@freespirit.com
www.freespirit.com

free spirit
PUBLiSHiNG®

Helping kids
help themselves®
since 1983

On Those Runaway Days

By Alison Feigh
Illustrated by Laura Logan

Dedicated to the children and youth of St. John in the Wilderness and
the Northern TEC Community in Minnesota.

A portion of the proceeds from sales of this book is being donated
by the author to the Jacob Wetterling Foundation (jwf.org).

Dear Parents and Caregivers,

When you were a child or teen, did you ever run away?

Running away is something many kids think about or try. As a small child, I attempted to run away from home, but since I was not yet allowed to cross the street, I just kept circling the block. My older brother followed me on his bike, on the instructions of my mom, and we kept circling until I calmed down. Sadly, not all children are just walking off a temper tantrum. They may be trying to find a solution to a serious problem, often an adult problem that has been placed in their laps.

When children are faced with problems at school or high-stress family changes such as divorce, abuse, the loss of a loved one, frustration, or anger, they may see running away as the means to fix things instead of what it truly is—a dangerous way to avoid working out a problem.

This book illustrates the importance of finding an adult to help when the easiest solution seems to be to run from the problem. It demonstrates to kids how impossible it is to try to solve big problems all by themselves. We want children to seek out adults to help them in situations where they feel unsafe, afraid, or angry. Adults are taught to seek out help when life gets too hard; we owe the same coping skills to our children.

It is my hope that by helping young children learn to seek out trustworthy support when things are frightening or overwhelming, we will reduce the likelihood of runaway behavior as children grow older. In so doing, we help kids know that they're special, that they deserve to be safe, and that there are adults who want to see them grow up emotionally healthy and strong.

When your kids face those runaway days, be sure they know that no problem is bigger than your love for them, and that you're here to help.

Alison Feigh

2

I am having a day when my problems seem very big ... and I feel angry, worried, and very small.

I wonder if it would be easier to just
run away from the problems and start fresh in a new place.

Right now, it feels like things would be better if I were somewhere else.

5

It feels like I am carrying a backpack stuffed with problems that I can't fix. I imagine that if I run away, the big problems will go away, too.

6

I take a few steps, but the backpack of problems is still there.

I run around in circles,
but my body hurts
from all the weight.

8

So, I stop running and
sit down under a tree.

I take a deep breath
and put my hands
behind my head.

10

I remember that Dad told me I have a one-of-a-kind brain that can dream big dreams and make good choices.

I take another
deep breath and
rub my eyes.

12

I know I can look for adults I trust who can help me deal
with my problems and lighten my load.

As I put my hand over
my mouth, I remember
to slow down my breathing.

I can feel myself calming
down, and I take
another deep breath.

14

I also know that talking about how I feel is part of making these big problems seem a bit smaller.

I put my hand over
my pounding heart,
and I think of all
the people I love.

16

Sometimes just taking time to remember I am loved
is enough to bring the smile back to my face.

My hands move down to my stomach, which is slowly starting to untie itself from the knots that were there a few minutes ago.

I know one thing I can always count on is my gut instinct—that "uh-oh" feeling I have in my stomach when there is a problem.

When I feel scared or upset, that "uh-oh" feeling starts inside me. It's a signal that reminds me to get out of the situation right away and find an adult I trust.

My "uh-oh" feeling is telling me this is one of those times. I need to stop running away and talk about how I feel.

The easiest person for
me to talk with is my mom.
I let my legs carry me
and my problems to
my mom, and I sit down
beside her.

I talk to Mom about this
runaway kind of day. She listens quietly
and lets me get out all my feelings. I tell
her about my backpack full of problems
and how angry it makes me feel.

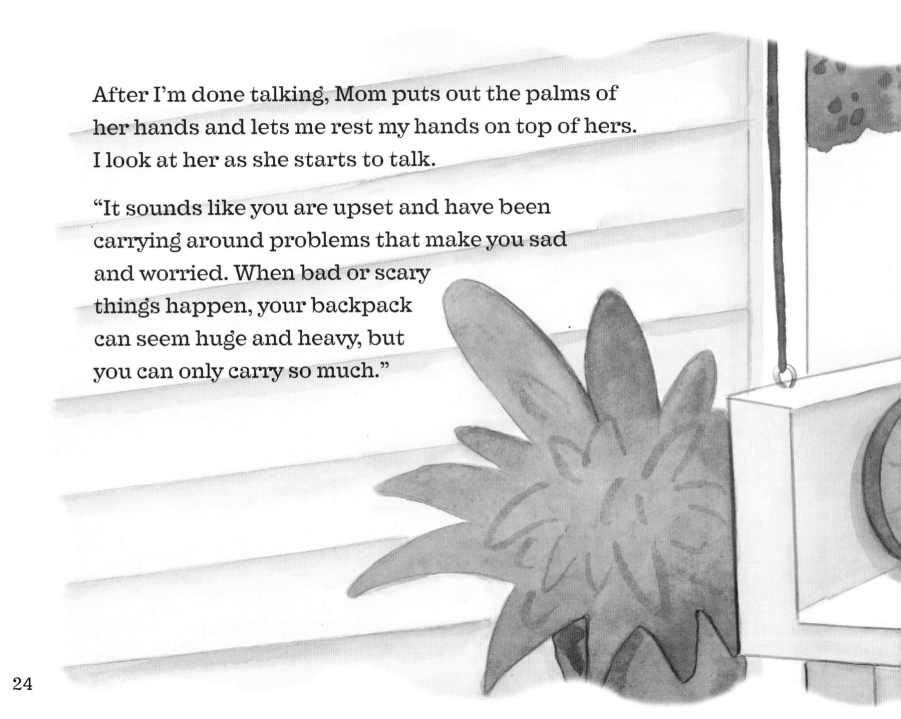

After I'm done talking, Mom puts out the palms of
her hands and lets me rest my hands on top of hers.
I look at her as she starts to talk.

"It sounds like you are upset and have been
carrying around problems that make you sad
and worried. When bad or scary
things happen, your backpack
can seem huge and heavy, but
you can only carry so much."

"I'm glad you came and talked to me about how you're feeling, because now we can unpack this backpack of problems, and solve them together."

I am a smart and unique person who deserves to be safe.
I have tools, like my head and my heart, to help me when things
get frightening or too stressful.

I also know that
having two heads,
two hearts, and
four hands to tackle
a problem can make
a world of difference.

My world is starting
to feel hopeful
and friendly again.

Personal Safety Tips

Most kids who run away do so because of family problems. One statistic says that one in seven kids ages 10 to 18 will run away at some point. If you challenge kids to name a problem that would get better by running away, they will likely be hard-pressed to give one good example. Even in cases where the child's home is not a safe place, the best thing for the child is to get help from other adults outside the home to address the problem. All children may not have access to a loving network of family grown-ups, but they should have access to teachers, principals, or a school nurse. Asking for help can be a scary thing, but it is far less scary than the alternative. Running away is not a romantic fantasy or a thrilling adventure—it is a dangerous way to avoid a problem. Running away always adds a whole new set of problems on top of the ones a young person is already experiencing.

Use this book to give children a powerful set of coping tools to use when facing a problem. Help kids keep a temporary problem from growing into something bigger by encouraging them to:

- use calming breathing whenever they feel anxious or afraid

- listen to their gut feelings

- think hard about making good choices

- seek out adults they trust (help them make a list of names, phone numbers, and email addresses)

- talk out the problem with caring adults

- remember they are surrounded by people who love them

Using these tools can be a powerful way to lift the weighty problems that life sometimes piles on our children's backs.

Sometimes the world we live in is not kind to our children. Sometimes we are not kind to our children. Children can blame themselves for divorce, abuse, or other family trauma. If an adult problem has entered into children's lives, tell them directly that it is not their fault. And remember to tell your children that they are loved unconditionally and that no problem is bigger than your love for them. If we raise children who know how to ask for help, they will know the importance of seeking out quality support on those runaway days.

Acknowledgments

Thank you to everyone who shared their expertise and resources in developing this project, especially Bridget Gambaniani; Max Stevenson; Rachel Babbitt; Lori Wiese-Parks of Gray, Plant, and Mooty Law Firm; and John Kober and the staff of Free Spirit Publishing.

Thank you to Nancy Sabin, executive director of the Jacob Wetterling Foundation, and to all of my wonderful past and present colleagues who work hard to make the world a safer place for children.

Thank you to Jerry and Patty Wetterling for cofounding the Jacob Wetterling Foundation in 1990. The Wetterling family members are each wonderful examples of what "hope" really means.

Thank you to my family who nurtured my creativity and taught me the importance of being part of the solution.

Other Great Books from Free Spirit

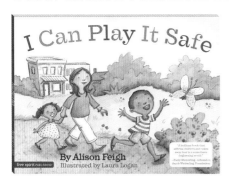

I Can Play It Safe

by Alison Feigh, illustrated by Laura Logan

Written by an expert in child safety, this full-color picture book teaches kids (and helps adults reinforce) seven important rules to personal safety in a nonthreatening way. It covers topics like safe versus harmful secrets, safe versus harmful touches, and the importance of having a community of trusted adults to turn to for help. For ages 4–8. $14.95; Hardcover; 32 pp.; color illust.; 10" x 7½".

Kids Need to Be Safe
A Book for Children in Foster Care

by Julie Nelson, illustrated by Mary Gallagher

In simple words, this book explains why some kids move to foster homes, what foster parents do, and how kids might feel during foster care. The text makes it clear that the troubles in children's lives are not their fault, and they deserve to be safe. For ages 4–10. $9.95; Softcover, 32 pp.; color illust.; 9" x 9".

When I Feel Afraid

by Cheri J. Meiners, M.Ed.

Helps children understand their fears, teaches simple coping skills, and encourages children to talk with trusted adults. One of 14 books in the Learning to Get Along® series. For ages 4–8. $10.95; Softcover; 40 pp.; color illust.; 9" x 9".

To place an order or to request a free catalog of Self-Help for Kids® and Self-Help for Teens® materials, please write, call, email, or visit our Web site:

Free Spirit Publishing Inc. • 217 Fifth Avenue North • Suite 200 • Minneapolis, MN 55401
toll-free 800.735.7323 • local 612.338.2068 • fax 612.337.5050 • help4kids@freespirit.com • www.freespirit.com